The Real You
Discovering Your God-Given Identity

Pastor Eddie J. Scarbrough

Scripture quotations marked (NKJV) are taken from the New King James Version®. Copyright © 1982 by Thomas Nelson. Used by permission. All rights reserved.

Scripture quotations marked TPT are from The Passion Translation®. Copyright © 2017, 2018, 2020 by Passion & Fire Ministries, Inc. Used by permission. All rights reserved. ThePassionTranslation.com.

THE REAL YOU- Discovering Your God-Given Identity.

Copyright © 2024 All rights reserved—Eddie J. Scarbrough

No part of this book may be reproduced or transmitted in any form or by any means, graphic, electronic, or mechanical, including photocopying, recording, taping, or by an information storage retrieval system without the written permission of the publisher.

Please direct all copyright inquiries to:
vscarbroughbtwf@gmail.com

Paperback ISBN: 978-0-9995498-8-9

Printed in the United States.

ACKNOWLEDGEMENTS

Thank You!

First, I would like to thank my Heavenly Father for creating me in His image and likeness and for giving me the inspiration to write this book. To my amazing wife Val Scarbrough, my children Stajjia, Zekee and Rod, along with my many grandchildren for being my biggest supporters in everything God has called and created me to be here in the earth. I love you with all my heart! I would like to thank the greatest church on the planet, Transforming Life Church Charlotte, and all our covenant partners for being students and doers of God's word. People like you make preaching and teaching the Gospel easy. To my mother, Brenda Scarbrough, for choosing to be a gateway by giving birth to me and allowing me to use her body as an incubator to love me to life. "I LOVE YOU MOMA (rest in heaven)!!" To my amazing mother-in-love, Olivia Bush, thank you and your friends (prayer partners) for praying me out of a very dark time in my life (I love you). Last, but certainly not least, to my awesome Pastors and Apostles Tony & Cynthia Brazelton for helping me to see who I really am in Christ Jesus. And developing me to be the man of faith I am today. I love you and words cannot express my appreciation for all you have done for me, my family, and our ministry.

Table of Contents

Foreword 6

Introduction 9

The Right Image 12

Citizen of Another World.. 20

Who's Ruling Who? 29

The Re-Birth 34

Jesus - Our Super Model... 42

Mind Reset 48

Your Personal Assistant 52

What Did Daddy Say About You? 58

Greater Works 64

Operating From Another World 71

Divinity -vs- Humanity.. 78

Confessions:... 88

FOREWORD

One of the biggest crimes in our society is identity theft. I believe it's one of the biggest crimes in the Body of Christ as well. I believe *The Real You* will put you on the path to discover who you are as well as your place in this world and in the Kingdom.

The Word of God reveals your true identity because the Word of God is meant to be relational. It's what God wants to be to you, so you know what you should be in every situation and circumstance. When you know who you are, you know what you should be personally, relationally, emotionally, mentally, financially and spiritually. Every time you hear the Word of God; God is unveiling some aspect about you.

The Word teaches us that we were created in the image and the likeness of God; we are of the God class of being.

We are a reflection of who HE IS which means we have inherited some aspects of His identity. Your existence on the earth is not ordinary. You are not the result of a mass production. You are unique and you will find your identity when you embrace who He made you to be. King David said, "I am fearfully and wonderfully made; marvelous are your works." David wasn't being arrogant; he was embracing his unique identity. David went on to say, "this is the Lord's doing and it is marvelous in our eyes."

It's through the finished work of Jesus Christ we get to walk in our God given identity. It's imperative that we embrace the reality that is communicated in the Gospels. The Apostle Paul revealed to us in Galatians 2:20 TPT, *"My old identity has been co-crucified with Messiah and no longer lives; for the nails of his cross crucified me with him. And now the essence of this new life is no longer mine, for the Anointed One lives his life through me— we live in union as one! My new life is empowered by the faith of the Son of God who loves me so much that he gave himself for me, and dispenses his life into mine!"* 1 John 4:17 declares, *"as Jesus is so are we in this world"*. That is our real identity.

2 Corinthians 5:16-17 (AMPC) states, *"Consequently, from now on we estimate and regard no one from a [purely] human point of view [in terms of natural standards of value]. [No] even though we once did estimate Christ from a human viewpoint and as a man, yet now [we have such knowledge of Him that] we know Him no longer [in terms of the flesh]. Therefore if any person is [ingrafted] in Christ (the Messiah) he is a new creation (a new creature*

altogether); the old [previous moral and spiritual condition] has passed away. Behold, the fresh and new has come!"

In this book, *The Real You* by Eddie Scarbrough, you'll discover your true identity, who God created you to be and then walk in your purpose. In Proverbs 3:21 (TPT), we are told that we are empowered by wisdom and purpose.

"My child, never drift off course from these two goals for your life: to walk in wisdom and to discover your purpose. Don't ever forget how they empower you."

When you are empowered, you will walk in the real you.

Walking with Pastor Eddie's personal life journey in this book will help you to discover where the enemy may have deceived you and now you can walk out of that illusion (something that deceives by producing a false or misleading impression of reality) and into your true self. Your mind will be renewed, and you will see yourself the way God created you and take your place in the Kingdom as a true son of God - *The Real You*!

Apostle Tony Brazelton
Victory Christian Ministries International

INTRODUCTION

To the person about to read this book, you are about to take a journey that will open your eyes to who you really are (THE REAL YOU)! Within the pages of this book are secrets through which God will reveal your real identity. You must approach this subject with an open mind to capture all God has for you where your heavenly citizenship is concerned.

I believe the contents in this message are something the devil does not want released into the lives of God's children, because he knows once we realize the power we possess through our Heavenly Father, nothing will be impossible to us (GLORY)!!! As you continue to read, it is my prayer your God given potential will begin to rumble and eventually explode in you and out of you, affecting everything and anything around you. *THE REAL YOU* is a game changer!

For you to grasp everything God has said to you, and about you, it is imperative that you cast down all religious thoughts that will try to enter your mind. This book was ordained to reintroduce you to who you really are. You see, many people make the statement "I KNOW WHO I AM" when in actuality nothing could be further from the truth. Most people identify more with who they are based on what their birth certificate that is sitting in some office says about them, or who their earthly father and mother called them. Through the pages of this book, you will discover God's original design for you because He is your original designer. You see, your mother may have given birth to you, but she did not design you. So, ladies and gentlemen, get comfortable as I introduced you to "*THE REAL YOU*"!

Chapter 1
THE RIGHT IMAGE

Then God said, "Let Us make man in Our image…"

Looking back over my life, I realize what a skewed view I had of myself. First, I had given my environment permission to paint a picture in my mind that was totally contradicting who God had created me to be. The images implanted in my mind and spirit were full of falsities that distracted me and filled my eyes with spiritual cataracts that left me blinded to who I really am in God. Then as I consistently studied the word of God, and implemented a steady regimen of prayer and fasting, God began to paint on the canvas of my imagination "*The Right Image*" with much bigger brush strokes that totally wiped out all the negative images I allowed my environment to foster in my mind.

As we begin this journey in finding out about *"The Real You,"* we must first discover *"The Right Image"* of who God created you and I to be. Let me start by saying the first place that Satan attacked Adam and Jesus was with their identity. This was a ploy to get them to question who God had created them to be and how He created them to function here in the earth. So, we should not be surprised when he uses the same tactics to try to confuse us when it comes to our true identity.

You see, it is very important that you see yourself as a perfect reflection of who God is. This is one area where Adam literally dropped the ball. Genesis 3:1-7 (NKJV) **says,** *"Now the serpent was more cunning than any beast of the field which the LORD God had made. And he said to the woman, "Has God indeed said, 'You shall not eat of every tree of the garden'?"*

*And the woman said to the serpent, "We may eat the fruit of the trees of the garden; but of the fruit of the tree which is in the midst of the garden, God has said, 'You shall not eat it, nor shall you touch it, lest you die.'" Then the serpent said to the woman, "**You will not surely die. For God knows that in the day you eat of it (YOUR EYES WILL BE OPENED), (AND YOU WILL BE LIKE GOD), knowing good and evil.**" So, when the woman saw that the tree was good for food, that it was pleasant to the eyes, and a tree desirable to make one wise, she took of its fruit and ate. She also gave to her husband with her, and he ate. Then the eyes of both of them were opened, and they knew that they were naked; and they sewed fig leaves together and made themselves coverings."* – (emphasis added by the author)

If you notice in bold print, the Devil made two statements. The first statement he made was (*"…**YOUR EYES WILL BE OPENED…**"*)

when in actuality they became blinded to who they really were when they ate the forbidden fruit. So, here we see the Devil use reverse psychology to move Adam and Eve away from their true identity! Their eyes were already open to who they were in God and the Devil knew that.

The second statement he made was, ("...***AND YOU WILL BE LIKE GOD...***"). When in fact, according to Genesis 1:26-28, they were already just like God. They were the spitting image of their Heavenly Father.

"Then God said, "Let Us make man in Our image, according to Our likeness; let them have dominion over the fish of the sea, over the birds of the air, and over the cattle, over all the earth and over every creeping thing that creeps on the earth." So, God created man in His own image; in the image of God He created him; male and female, He created them. Then God blessed them, and God said to them, "Be fruitful and multiply; fill the earth and subdue

it; have dominion over the fish of the sea, over the birds of the air, and over every living thing that moves on the earth. (Genesis 1:26-28 NKJV)

The whole reason God created His man was so His man could experience the good life all his life, just like his Heavenly Father. You see, that is why it is so important that we get the right image of who we are in Christ Jesus. Jesus' mind was so locked into knowing that He was equal with His Father, or should I say, made in God's image, He was able to accomplish everything that He was sent here to accomplish. Jesus did not think that it was dysfunctional to function just like His Daddy or to look like Him. GLORY TO GOD!!!!

If we look closely at the scripture, we will see just how Jesus saw Himself when it came to the image He was created in. Philippians 2:5-6 (NKJV) says, *"Let this mind be in you which was also in Christ Jesus, who, being in the form of God, did not consider it robbery to be equal with God."* What am I saying? This is the same mindset we all should have, so we will have the "RIGHT IMAGE" of who we are.

You know, having the right image of yourself is key to living a successful, victorious, and prosperous life. Some people say image is not everything. However, having the right image is paramount to fulfilling your purpose here in the earth. Do not allow the Devil to cause you to have a "wicker" view or image of yourself. The word "wicker" means "twisted". This is where the idea of wicker furniture comes from. Wicker furniture is furniture that is twisted. In a nutshell, do not allow the Devil to twist the truth about whose image you were duplicated from. Listen, you are a perfect *duplication* of God Himself!

Most of us have looked into mirrors all our lives. So, I believe it is safe to say we have a photographic memory when it comes to knowing how we look without looking at our reflection. Our image of ourselves has been imprinted in our mind and when we look at our reflection, if something is out of order, it is innate in us to immediately fix it. Well, the word of God is a spiritual mirror that reflects our image in God. This is a perfect description to explain who you look like.

2 Corinthians 3:18 (NLT) says, *"So all of us who have had that veil removed can see and reflect the glory of the Lord. And the Lord—who is the Spirit—makes us more and more like him as we are changed into his glorious image."*

We must get to the place where we are fully convinced that we have God's DNA running through our veins. That's right, God's DNA, not your earthly father and mother's DNA only. God said before He formed you in the womb, He knew you. So, I believe it is safe to say God's description of your identity is very accurate in giving you a clear picture of *The Real You*.

I'm not sure if you know it or not, but you are a very powerful person! You are a super Man/Woman called to do great things here in the earth. It is very important that you see yourself right. Because when you see yourself right, you will tap into everything God has made available to you.

Reading the word of God is very beneficial in helping you become acquainted with who you are.

Chapter 2
CITIZEN OF ANOTHER WORLD

"In the World, But Not of It…"

Years ago, I remember periodically hearing a quote by Oliver Wendell Holmes that says, "*NEVER BE SO HEAVENLY MINDED, YOU'RE NO EARTHLY GOOD!*"

Well, I chose to believe the opposite. In fact, I became the kind of person who believes if I am Heavenly minded first, surely, I can bring some good into the earth.

Colossians 3:1-4 NKJV says, *"If then you were raised with Christ, seek those things which are above, where Christ is, sitting at the right hand of God. Set your mind on things above, not on things on the earth. For you died, and your life is hidden with Christ in God. When Christ who is our life appears, then you also will appear with Him in glory."*

I thought at one time I was only a citizen of this corrupt world. And if truth be told, I was corrupting everything in my path. From a troubled teen to an adult, I was a menace to society. But thanks be to God! Today, I am sold out to Jesus! Today, I can confidently say I am a Kingdom of God citizen. I AM A CITIZEN OF ANOTHER WORLD!

"*We are in this world but not of this world…,*" is a profound statement in God's word that reveals to us we are citizens of another kingdom. Jesus made this truth known in John 17:16 KJV when He said, *"They are not of the world, even as I am not of the world."* This is evidence that we are from a place that transcends this earthly realm. *The Real You*

The Real You

has the ability to rise above or go beyond the normal limits of how this world functions. You have been equipped to triumph over the negative and restrictive influence of this world's system.

As a Christian, you should never get comfortable with what the world's system can offer you. You may ask, *"…why do you say that?"* I am glad you asked! You and I are ambassadors sent here by our Heavenly Father to complete our assignment here in the earth. God, the Father, never intended for us to get comfortable and settle for just existing in this earth realm, but it is our duty to be His representatives and help reconcile all of humanity back to Himself. The more I study our true identity in Christ, the more I am becoming aware of our true power and our true citizenship.

Child of God, we must understand that we have all of Heaven supporting and backing us up. Heaven is aiding and assisting us so we can reach our known goal where the assignment God has placed on our life is concerned.

In the United States of America, we have what we call U.S. Embassies in different parts of the world. Each U.S. Embassy, although they are in other locations outside of America, are still lawfully considered as U.S. soil and the people they serve in them are U.S. citizens. So, what does that mean? That means every person inside each embassy is not operating according to the laws of the country where the Embassy is located, but they are under the laws and jurisdiction of the country (the United States of America) from which they came. I guess we can say it like this. *"They are citizens of another world!"*

Jeremiah 1:4-5 NKJV says, *"Then the word of the LORD came to me, saying: Before I formed you in the womb I knew you; Before you were born I sanctified you; I ordained you a prophet to the nations."*

When we were with God in Heaven before He sent us on our assignment to the earth, we had a relationship with Him. We must understand this is not our first time being alive. As a matter of fact, we were more alive in Heaven than we are right now. Just imagine, when we were in Heaven, there was no sickness, disease, sadness, hate, pain, defeat and/or any of the negative things we experience here in the earth. When we transitioned from Heaven to earth, we became subject to these things. However, the greater One lives on the inside of us and who we really are (THE REAL YOU) has power and authority over every negative influence that we may encounter.

Psalms 51:5 NKJV states, *"Behold, I was brought forth in iniquity, And in sin my mother conceived me."*

It was not until we crossed the threshold from Heaven into this earth realm, we became sinners. I am so thankful to God for sending His son,

Jesus, our elder brother, into the earth to take our sins upon Himself. He allowed His blood to be shed for us because, without the shedding of blood, there is no remission of sin. When Jesus died for us, and we accepted Him as our Lord and Savior, we became born again.

What does it mean to be born again? This does not mean you are born again physically, but your spirit "THE REAL YOU" has been re-created. Jesus traded places with us so we could become the righteousness of God. He became sin for us! GLORY TO GOD!!!!

John 3:1-21 NKJV says, *"There was a man of the Pharisees named Nicodemus, a ruler of the Jews. This man came to Jesus by night and said to Him, "Rabbi, we know that You are a teacher come from God; for no one can do these signs that You do unless God is with him." Jesus answered and said to him, "Most assuredly, I say to you, unless one is born again, he cannot see the kingdom of*

God." Nicodemus said to Him, "How can a man be born when he is old? Can he enter a second time into his mother's womb and be born?" Jesus answered, "Most assuredly, I say to you, unless one is born of water and the Spirit, he cannot enter the kingdom of God. That which is born of the flesh is flesh, and that which is born of the Spirit is spirit. Do not marvel that I said to you, 'You must be born again.' The wind blows where it wishes, and you hear the sound of it, but cannot tell where it comes from and where it goes. So is everyone who is born of the Spirit." Nicodemus answered and said to Him, "How can these things be?" Jesus answered and said to him, "Are you the teacher of Israel, and do not know these things? Most assuredly, I say to you, We speak what We know and testify what We have seen, and you do not receive Our witness. If I have told you earthly things and you do not believe, how will you believe if I tell you heavenly things? No one has ascended to heaven but He who came down from heaven, that is, the Son of Man who is in heaven.

And as Moses lifted up the serpent in the wilderness, even so must the Son of Man be lifted up, that whoever believes in Him should not perish but have eternal life. For God so loved the world that He gave His only begotten Son, that whoever believes in Him should not perish but have everlasting life. For God did not send His Son into the world to condemn the world, but that the world through Him might be saved. "He who believes in Him is not condemned; but he who does not believe is condemned already, because he has not believed in the name of the only begotten Son of God. And this is the condemnation, that the light has come into the world, and men loved darkness rather than light, because their deeds were evil. For everyone practicing evil hates the light and does not come to the light, lest his deeds should be exposed. But he who does the truth comes to the light, that his deeds may be clearly seen, that they have been done in God."

As I was thinking about being a "citizen of another world" it came to me that in the natural,

The Real You

I am a native of the state of Alabama although I now live in North Carolina. I have learned to appreciate the great state of North Carolina, not to mention my wife and I love the people here, but my roots will forever be in Alabama because that is where I am from. "ROLL TIDE", LOL!!! So likewise, I am thankful God sent me to this earth on assignment, yes assignment, but my roots will forever be in Heaven. You and I should never forget we are citizens of Heaven first, who happen to have temporary residence here in the earth. As a "citizen of another world," we must understand all our resources come from Heaven and are manifested here in the earth. In a nutshell, God, our Heavenly Father, is our source.

Chapter 3
WHO'S RULING WHO?

"I say then: Walk in the Spirit, and you shall not fulfill the lust of the flesh…"

Have you ever thought you were in full control of your life? Only to end up realizing you were totally out of control. Do not feel bad. I have been there before. There was a time in my life my flesh dominated and ruled every aspect of my life. That is until I learned better. It was almost like I had no say in the way my life was going. My flesh was literally the puppet master over my spirit. I could have just plastered an "out of order" sign across my chest. As we look at this chapter, God will reveal to you and me the proper order for our lives.

God makes a statement in His word that gives us the key to walking in true freedom from all distractions and devices of Satan himself. Galatians 5:16-18 NKJV states, *"I say then: Walk in the Spirit, and you shall not fulfill the lust of the flesh. For the flesh lusts against the Spirit, and the Spirit against the flesh; and these are contrary to one another, so that you do not do the things that you wish. But if you are led by the Spirit, you are not under the law."*

One thing we must understand is that Satan will always try to influence us to give in to the dictates of our carnal nature, which is our flesh. Which begs the question, "WHO IS RULING WHO"?

When God placed us in our mortal body, it was never in His plans for us to be dominated by the house we live in (the flesh). You and I are not the physical bodies we live in. Our body is the house we reside in, it is not who we are. As I stated earlier, *THE REAL YOU* is your spirit man.

We are all another speaking spirit, just like God. The only reason we have a physical flesh, blood, and bone body is because for us to legally operate in this natural realm, God had to create a house for us to live, otherwise known as our flesh suit. Let's look at it like this. In order for you and me to take a trip into space, we first need what is called a space suit. This suit would give us the capability to function and operate in a realm that our physical bodies were not created to operate in. So, likewise, the only way you and I can survive and operate here in the earth realm is to wear this earth suit God created for us.

This next statement is very important for us to understand. Without your spirit living in your physical body, your physical body cannot function. Your spirit was created to control and dictate to your flesh what it will and will not do. Your flesh was never created to control and dictate the actions of THE REAL YOU, your spirit man.

Often times, people find themselves more sensitive to what the flesh desires and totally ignore what their spirit man wants and needs. This is not the will of God for His children. He expects our spirit man to dominate every area of our life. Once we master this, no depression, sickness, disease, demonic attacks, and/or any other outside negative force can defeat us!

Listen, with everything in us, we must allow our spirit man (THE REAL YOU) to take the helm and steer our lives in the right direction. Your spirit man is always on the ready to take the lead, so whatever you do, do not override your spirit man by leaning to the understanding of the thought patterns of the flesh. Proverbs 3:5-6 NKJV says, *"Trust in the LORD with all your heart, And lean not on your own understanding; In all your ways acknowledge Him, And He shall direct your paths."* This is why it is paramount that we listen to our spirit and let our spirit "RULE" and lead our lives completely.

THE REAL YOU is a dominator, a champion, a warrior, and a "RULER"! So let him take his/her rightful place in your life and you will begin to see a major shift in every area of your life. Child of God, we must continue to remind ourselves who we are, especially in the world we live in today. There are so many things trying to dictate to us who we are and oppose our true identity in Christ Jesus, but we KNOW the truth and it is the truth that makes us free!

Chapter 4
THE RE-BIRTH

Growing up, I thought there was no way out of the life I chose to live. I had handed myself a life sentence and put the nails in the coffin of my life as if to tell myself, this is as far as you will go. I did not know that there was a re-birth awaiting me. I was living the life of a hamster on a wheel. Thank God one day I really heard the gospel of Jesus Christ and the sacrifice He made for me when He died on the cross for my sins. This was the message that snatched me off the hamster wheel that was leading nowhere into a life I would like to call the "Re-Birth".

You may be saying to yourself, what does "The Re-birth" mean? When Adam and Eve sinned, they did not die physically. However, they did die spiritually. They were separated from God, their Father. And because they were separated, that caused you and me to become separated from our Heavenly Father as well. So, the only way we could return to the family of God was to be born again. Therefore, we should be thankful to God for giving His only begotten son, Jesus, as a ransom for us. The Re-birth comes from us receiving Jesus as our Lord and Savior. Let's look at what the word of God has to say about it in John 3:3-7 NKJV:

"Jesus answered and said to him, "Most assuredly, I say to you, unless one is born again, he cannot see the kingdom of God." Nicodemus said to Him, "How can a man be born when he is old? Can he enter a second time into his mother's womb and be born?" Jesus answered, "Most

assuredly, I say to you, unless one is born of water and the Spirit, he cannot enter the kingdom of God. That which is born of the flesh is flesh, and that which is born of the Spirit is spirit. Do not marvel that I said to you, 'You must be born again."

Being born again re-introduces you to who you really are. Never forget, you are a spirit first. That is the real you. This process is so vital to every person who is born on this physical earth because it guarantees our citizenship in Heaven, which is where we all originally came from.

Before we came to this earth, we were all righteous, but once we entered this world, we were born into sin. That's why our spiritual re-birth is so important. This allows our spirit man to move to the forefront and navigate our life. *The Real You* (your spirit man) craves to be in full control of your life, so your re-birth gives your spirit man full advantage to do so.

I don't know about you, but I am so thankful God had a plan in place to help us rise to the occasion and totally walk into our true identity. Being born again is such a blessing to you and me because it helps us be and become all that God has called us to be. You see, our salvation is bigger than just going to Heaven. It also releases us to become who He created us to be and empowers us to live out our purpose that ensures the manifestation of His Kingdom in the Earth (THANK YOU JESUS)!

The re-birth transforms us from the inside out. A newly recreated spirit is the most valuable thing a person can possess. There is a newness that takes place that causes us to understand that something amazing happened to us. And that something is the saving power of Jesus Christ. I am so thankful Jesus died for all of mankind, because if He did not, we all would be as good as dead.

Jesus died so you and I do not have to spend an eternity in Hell separated from God! GLORY TO GOD!!!! Like many of you, I could not clearly see my way in life until I was born again. This door opened to help set my life on a path that has been very rewarding and fulfilling. If you notice, I did not say perfect because a fulfilling life is not void of life's challenges.

Let's talk about that for a moment. Being born again and having challenges is all a part of the process that helps us understand who we were re-born to be. You and I are children of the most-high God through the sacrifice of our Lord and Savior Jesus Christ. Our identity was locked up in Jesus until He was offered as a sacrificial seed that was planted and in-turn we were transformed into the very image of Christ.

One of my favorite scriptures is 2 Corinthians 5:17 KJV *"Therefore, if any man be in Christ, he is a new creature: old things are passed away; behold, all things are become new."* The re-birth strips us of the old and clothes us with the new, meaning "Jesus Christ." Our salvation is the reintroduction of our real selves to ourselves. Before the re-birth, we did not know who we are or whose we are.

If you are born again, take a moment to think back on the day you were saved. Do you remember how you felt and the joy that overwhelmed you? That's something we should never forget. Continue to remind yourself of that awesome moment and it will keep you from ever doubting your re-birth.

You are the apple of God's eye! Yes you! Your re-birth into God's Kingdom draws you closer to the inheritance that is laid up for you. Your status in God's family is royalty. Make sure to take full advantage of your re-birth. The Bible says we are kings and priests. So, our re-birth helps establish our kingship and our priesthood. What a wonderful position to be in and have a pedigree straight out of Heaven.

Did you know God is counting on you knowing who you are? Your re-birth signifies your place in God's heart. The only way God can operate legally here in the earth is through you and me. The only reason we are born into this earth is to carry out God's purpose for our lives. We need to make sure that we lock into the Kingdom of God because that's the family we are now a part of. Just think about that, we are children of the most-high God!!!!! GLORY!!!!!!

Today, it's my job to encourage you to take full advantage of your Kingdom citizenship. There is no such thing as you not having enough to make it in this life or being defeated. You have been birthed into wealth and victory. Walk and talk like the royalty you are. Make sure your mind is fixed on your heavenly inheritance. This is where your assurance in your re-birth remains solid.

Chapter 5
JESUS - OUR SUPER MODEL

My friend, I remember growing up in my hometown Tuscaloosa, Alabama and seeing a smorgasbord of different life models that shaped me into a product of the environment I was a part of. I tried to talk, walk, and live like some people around me. The runway of my environment had me mesmerized with the models that took the stage called my community. Do not get me wrong, I had good, bad, and ugly (I am not talking about physical characteristics) models all around me and they affected my life. Later in life, I took a deep dive into the word of God and had an encounter with Jesus that caused me to evaluate His life closely. As a result, I found myself wanting and practicing being more and more like Him. That is why I can say not only is He a model for me, but He is my "Super Model!"

Today, when we think about a supermodel, our minds immediately create an image of a man or woman we deem is beautiful based on their outward appearance only. However, when we look at Jesus as our supermodel, we should focus in on a man who knew who He was based on what was on the inside of Him.

I like to say it like this: *"Jesus modeled a message! He would often boldly state to those that were around Him, 'I and my father are one!!'"* Just like Jesus boldly declared that He is one with His father, we are now positioned to declare we are one with Christ. 1st John 4:17 KJV says, *"As He (Jesus) is so are we in this world."* In a nutshell, we should model everything that Jesus has and is displaying for us here in the earth.

You see, Jesus knew who He was while here in the earth, so He fully operated as God. Everywhere He went, He functioned in His God-given power and authority. Jesus was a dominator! The Bible even declares, right now He is seated in a place of authority at the right hand of God. I know this may be hard for some people to grasp in their mind, but everything Jesus did, you and I can do.

Every day we wake up, we should declare I am just like Jesus! I know religion has made us feel like this statement is blasphemy, but that could not be further from the truth. This should be our declaration of the truth that has been revealed to us about our identity in Christ, who is our super model.

Let me take this a little further. Believe it or not, Jesus is expecting us to outdo Him here in the earth and bring our Heavenly Father even more glory. I know you may say, what in the world are you talking about? Well, I am glad you asked. Here is scripture to help you better understand where I am coming from.

"Most assuredly, I say to you, he who believes in Me, the works that I do he will do also; and greater works than these he will do, because I go to My Father." John 14:12 (NKJV)

These words are straight from the mouth of Jesus. He is saying that He expects us to do what He has done and, to a greater magnitude, that we eclipse everything He ever accomplished. Now we never want to get it twisted! Without the greater one (Jesus) living on the inside of us, we cannot complete our mission here in the earth successfully.

The Real You

While Jesus was here in the earth, He performed many miracles. He healed the sick, raised the dead, open blinded eyes, and cast out demons throughout the duration of His earthly ministry. I am simply saying we must be determined to do the same and more. Jesus came to set the captives free, so this should also be the foundation of our ministry and who we are in Him. I would like to challenge you and myself to be very diligent in making sure we step into who we really are and embrace the fact that we are sons and daughters of an almighty God and a part of the body of Christ.

I am reminded by Holy Spirit that Jesus never had a challenge He did not conquer. When He would encounter someone who was sick or maybe even dead, He never became rattled. In fact, He was convinced about who He was and the authority He possessed. The first miracle He performed was turning water into wine at a wedding. Now in the natural that does not make sense, but when you know who you really are, and the power and authority you have been given by your Heavenly Father, you will learn to push past the opinions of people. You will learn to go with the flow and follow the model that Jesus has put in place for each of us.

Chapter 6
MIND RESET

Let This Mind Be in You...

As a young teenager, I had a very warped way of thinking. My mind was so jacked up, I began doing things that not only disappointed my parents, but I am quite sure it disappointed God as well. The way I was thinking and acting was totally unacceptable in so many ways. I wish I could go back and change some things I did because of my corrupt thinking, but that is impossible. One thing I found out later in life is I could have a "Mind Re-set" based on what I received from God's word. The more I studied His word, the more I noticed a "Mind Re-set" was taking place for me. Hallelujah!!!!!

When I was growing up, there was a saying, "*A MIND is a terrible thing to waste.*" This is the absolute truth! How we think will guide our lives. Our mind is our internal navigation system. With that being said, most of us have to have our minds reset and renewed because of bad teaching and downloads. Our mind is the central command center for our life. It is imperative that we remember our mind is a spirit according to Ephesians 4:23 (NKJV) which says, *"…and be renewed in the spirit of your mind."*

This is a sign that we must make a conscious choice to have our minds reset. We reset many things in our lives we deem important to us. Things like our computer, cell phone, television and even the check engine light in our cars. So surely, we should renew or rest our minds. You will never discover *The Real You* without first renewing your mind.

If you and I are going to walk in all that God has called us to walk in, we must think like Jesus and understand we are one with our Heavenly Father. God Himself put His spirit inside of each of us and that includes having the ability to think on His level. However, so many of us are convinced that is not possible. Philippians 2:5 (NKJV) says, *"Let this mind be in you which was also in Christ Jesus."* Jesus had the mind of God, so this scripture proves that we too have the ability to think like God.

We must have a mind-over-matter approach to every situation in life. 2 Corinthians 4:18 (NKJV) says, *"…while we do not look at the things which are seen, but at the things which are not seen. For the things which are seen are temporary, but the things which are not seen are eternal."* Sometimes our minds will play tricks on us based on what our eyes see. We must continue to think on the things God has instructed us to think on, just as He outlined in Philippians 4:8-9 NKJV.

"Finally, brethren, whatever things are true, whatever things are noble, whatever things are just, whatever things are pure, whatever things are lovely, whatever things are of good report, if there is any virtue and if there is anything praiseworthy—meditate on these things. The things which you learned and received and heard and saw in me, these do, and the God of peace will be with you."

Chapter 7
YOUR PERSONAL ASSISTANT
The Helper

It has been said since I was a little child, and even today, I have an independent spirit. In some ways, this can be a good thing, but on the other hand, it has been detrimental to my life on countless occasions. What do I mean by that? Well, I was not a good listener. It was not an attribute of someone like me who has an independent spirit. I did not like listening to authority figures at all, including my parents. Bad idea young people! As I have gotten older, that has truly changed in my life. Now, I do all I can to follow proper authority. First and foremost, my leading authority is Holy Spirit, "My Personal Assistant."

Let me start out by saying I love Holy Spirit! He is my friend and I am so thankful Jesus chose to leave this earth so the Comforter could come. Holy Spirit is here in the earth to help train you and me where our spirit man is concerned; to help navigate, shape, and mold *The Real You*. You and I are both wrapped in a flesh suit that houses our spirit, so Holy Spirit's assignment is to help us develop our spirit to the point our spirit man is driving our flesh and not our flesh driving our spirit man.

Earlier I mentioned Holy Spirit is "My Personal Assistant." Now, I would like to define for you what that means. An assistant is a person who helps someone, especially a person whose job is to help another person to do work. You see, Holy

Spirit's job is to help *The Real You* do the work of the Father here in the earth realm. In Luke 2:49 NKJV, Jesus' earthly father and mother thought He was lost for several days, and this is what Jesus said to them, *"Why did you seek Me? Did you not know that I must be about My Father's business?"*

That should be our mandate here in the earth, "we must be about our Heavenly Father's business." But there is one thing we should be mindful of and that is we need Holy Spirit to assist us.

"If you love Me, keep My commandments. And I will pray the Father, and He will give you another Helper, that He may abide with you forever — the Spirit of truth, whom the world cannot receive, because it neither sees Him nor knows Him; but you know Him, for He dwells with you and will be in you. I will not leave you orphans; I will come to you." -John 14:15-18 NKJV

Jesus also needed Holy Spirit to come and assist Him when He started His earthly ministry.

"Then Jesus was led up by the Spirit into the wilderness to be tempted by the Devil. And when He had fasted forty days and forty nights, afterward He was hungry. Now when the tempter came to Him, he said, "If You are the Son of God, command that these stones become bread." But He answered and said, "It is written, 'Man shall not live by bread alone, but by every word that proceeds from the mouth of God." -Matthew 4:1-4 NKJV

It was Holy Spirit that empowered Jesus to resist the temptation of the Devil. One thing is for sure, the Devil will come to all of us during different seasons in life to tempt us to veer away from our God-given assignment here in the earth. That is why it is so important for us to totally lean and depend on our personal assistant, Holy Spirit, who gives us the strength to walk away from anyone or anything that does not benefit us in reaching our known goal in the Kingdom of God.

I do not know about you, but I don't know what I would do without Holy Spirit in my life. Our spirit man yearns to connect with Holy Spirit more than anything in this world! You and I were not called to function in this world alone. Holy Spirit assists us by giving us "POWER!" Listen to what Jesus had to say about Him in Acts 1:4-8 NKJV:

"And being assembled together with them, He commanded them not to depart from Jerusalem, but to wait for the Promise of the Father, "which," He said, "you have heard from Me; for John truly baptized with water, but you shall be baptized with the Holy Spirit not many days from now." Therefore, when they had come together, they asked Him, saying, "Lord, will You at this time restore the kingdom to Israel?" And He said to them, "It is not for

you to know times or seasons which the Father has put in His own authority. But you shall receive power when the Holy Spirit has come upon you; and you shall be witnesses to Me in Jerusalem, and in all Judea and Samaria, and to the end of the earth."

Chapter 8
WHAT DID DADDY SAY ABOUT YOU?

As I lean into this chapter, I am reminded of my earthly daddy, Willie Butler (RIH), who God blessed my brother and I with after a tragic car accident took our biological father, Eddie Billups', life (RIH) about 30 days before I was born. My earthly daddy was by no means a perfect man, but he was a great provider and always spent quality time with my brother and me. I remember he would always speak positively about us, even though we did not always do positive things. I would always hear him speak from a place as if to say my sons can do anything. I am not sure if he really knew what he said about us built us up to where we knew nothing was impossible for us. Well likewise, my Heavenly Father (Daddy God) has spoken nothing but life and possibility over you and me. The thing is, we have to shut out every negative word that has ever been spoken over us and lean into what our Heavenly Daddy has said and is saying about us.

As God's greatest creation, we all should know what He has spoken concerning us. I like to view God the Father as my daddy because that is who He is to me. I love to read His word to see exactly what He said concerning me. But my question to you is, what did Daddy say about you? Not sure? Let me tell you! Daddy (God) has only spoken life words concerning you and me so that we will come into the full knowledge and image of who He created us to be.

The Real You

Sometimes we can get caught up listening to everything that the Devil is saying about us until it overshadows what our Heavenly Father has already spoken over us. I like to tell people this; *"…if the Devil ever tells you something, believe the opposite."*

Psalms 139:13-15 NKJV is a scripture that gives us one example of what Daddy says about us: *"For You formed my inward parts; You covered me in my mother's womb. I will praise You, for I am fearfully and wonderfully made; Marvelous are Your works, And that my soul knows very well. My frame was not hidden from You, When I was made in secret, And skillfully wrought in the lowest parts of the earth."*

It is very important that you and I continue to investigate and explore the word of God to find every treasure in God's word that shows us exactly what has been released over our lives. This is imperative in helping us speak the right things over our own life. Confessing the word of God over our own life causes supernatural manifestation to show up in our life in a great way. When we find out what Daddy (God) has said about us, we need to receive it daily, proclaim it, and live by it.

Did you know we have been ordained by Daddy (God) as Kings and Priests? That's right, we have been placed in a position of power and authority. Daddy (God) has placed His stamp of approval on our lives. Revelation 5:9-10 NKJV tells us: *"And they sang a new song, saying: 'You are worthy to take the scroll, And to open its seals; For You were slain, And have redeemed us to God by Your blood Out of every tribe and tongue and people and nation, And have made us kings and priests to our God; And we shall reign on the earth.'…"*

Wow! Did you hear that? Not only are we kings and priests, but we have also been called to REIGN on the EARTH! GLORY TO GOD!!! That is what I am trying to make very clear here. There are so many outstanding things Daddy (God) has said about you, and the word of God gives us in-depth descriptions of who we are that exposes *The Real You*!

We can look at it like this. Some people like to read food packages to see what the food contains before they consume it. Well, the word of God says you and I are fearfully and wonderfully made. God is saying He knows exactly what He put in us. He knows what is in the packaging. He knows exactly what is in you and I. Everything that is in Him is in us (Hallelujah)!! This journey of life has been set for us by Daddy (God).

Eddie J. Scarbrough

"Remember the former things of old, For I am God, and there is no other; I am God, and there is none like Me, Declaring the end from the beginning, And from ancient times things that are not yet done, Saying, 'My counsel shall stand, And I will do all My pleasure.'" -Isaiah 46:9-10 NKJV

If we as God's children spent more time with Him in prayer and reading His word, He will have a Daddy to son/daughter talk with us that will open our eyes to everything He has spoken concerning us.

Chapter 9
GREATER WORKS

You know, at one time in my life I did not realize I was destined for greater. I literally thought the only thing I would do was to live the street life hustling and be great in the eyes of those who were doing the same thing I was. The things I saw day in and day out blinded me to the possibilities available to me. It is so liberating to know Jesus has set the course for you and me to do "Greater Works" here in the earth all for the Glory of God. I am excited! How about you? Let's go!

I know. This does not make any sense to our natural mind. How can this be? Who can do greater works than JESUS!? Well, according to the word of God, *The Real You* can. You see, Jesus came to be an example to us to reveal not only who we are but also our ability to operate as gods here in the earth. And guess what, to do it on a greater level than He did. The word of God promises in Luke 10:19 NKJV that Jesus did not leave us on the earth and in this world powerless. *"Behold, I give you the authority to trample on serpents and scorpions, and over all the power of the enemy, and nothing shall by any means hurt you."*

This is our power pellet, but it is up to you and me to swallow it, digest it, believe it, and operate in it. We must be willing to take up this mantle and move forward in the greater works realm so the Kingdom of God can dominate here in this world. The greater works were given to us so we can bring glory to God's name.

The greater works I am speaking of are not given to draw people to us, but to draw them to God and His Kingdom. Yes, we are made in God's image and likeness (The Real You), and there are many benefits available to us because of who our daddy is. However, the greater works are not meant for our own self/personal gain, but to further the Kingdom of God.

Listen, my friend! I encourage you to wake up every day expecting God to use *The Real You* to do greater works. The challenge is that some of us do not feel like we are worthy of being used by God to do greater works because of some things we have done in our past. I have good news for you! If Jesus is your Lord and Savior, He made you (The Real You) worthy! Thank you, Jesus!!!

We must grab hold of the same confidence Jesus had when He revealed to the people that He had authority to operate just like His Heavenly Father here in the earth. Listen to what Jesus had to say:

"For the Father loves the Son, and shows Him all things that He Himself does; and He will show Him greater works than these, that you may marvel. For as the Father raises the dead and gives life to them, even so the Son gives life to whom He will." John 5:20-21 NKJV

What was Jesus saying? He was saying, "like Father, like son." He was saying to the people, you thought the works I have done up to this point were something. You have not seen anything yet! Which is why the word of God tells us in John 14:21-14 NKJV that we shall do even greater works than what Jesus did. *"Most assuredly, I say to you, he who believes in Me, the works that I do he will do also; and greater works than these he will do, because I go to My Father. And whatever you ask in My name, that I will do, that the Father may be glorified in the Son. If you ask anything in My name, I will do it."*

We have the access code to whatever we need in this world. All our resources are locked up in the name of Jesus. Jesus said if we ask anything in His name, He will do it for us. This is where the greater works realm is located for us. See *The Real You* knows the ability you have in and through Christ Jesus, but the house you and I live in (the flesh) has no clue as to the investment that has been made in us to carry out what God has called and ordained us to do.

Although Jesus had a flesh, blood, and bone body like we do, when He was taking care of the works of the Kingdom, He always operated in His what I like to call GOD-SHIP! The Real You that shall do greater works is your GOD-SHIP! This is the part of you and me that has the right and the ability to function just like gods in the earth. We are little g's! We are God's offspring with God's DNA! To make it plain, we can say it like this: the same stuff that is on the inside of God is on the inside of us! Hallelujah!

Let's talk about Jesus some more. I love Jesus and I love talking about Him! Every time I read in God's word about all the wonderful and mighty works Jesus did, I am tempted to ask, *"how can we top that?"* Especially when I read scriptures like John 20:30-31 and John 21:25:

"And truly Jesus did many other signs in the presence of His disciples, which are not written in this book; but these are written that you may believe that Jesus is the Christ, the Son of God, and that believing you may have life in His name." -John 20:30-31 NKJV

"And there are also many other things that Jesus did, which if they were written one by one, I suppose that even the world itself could not contain the books that would be written. Amen." -John 21:25 NKJV

WOW! Everything Jesus did was not even recorded and Jesus Himself said that you and I will do greater works. So, let's make up our minds that we are going to embrace the greater works position. This is where God ordained us to be and to operate. I believe God is recording every work we perform on behalf of His Kingdom. We should yield to this assignment and function fully in what we know will bring our Heavenly Father glory. When we graduate to the greater works level, it says to Him we submit completely and totally to Him.

Let's admit, this world could use the greater works of God flowing through it. I believe as Christians, God is depending on us to function as Kingdom Citizens here in the earth. Isn't that wonderful!? We get the honor of representing a system that will never be broken!

Chapter 10
OPERATING FROM ANOTHER WORLD

Seated in Heavenly Places

I remember when I truly started working my faith and believing God on another level. It was like I had entered a zone where I knew whatever I ask God for, He would surely bring it to pass in my life. My faith was unshakeable, so much so that as soon as I spoke it and released it out of my mouth, it would not delay in manifesting. I was operating from another world. This is the place I strive to continue to camp out in. Father God, continue to allow Your grace to be upon my life, so I will always know that I operate from another place beyond this world.

I was sitting and pondering on our position in Christ Jesus, and it hit me really strongly that we are in a position of authority, power, and preeminence. I never could see that years ago, although I have been saved since the age of eight years old. This particular day, it hit me that you and I have the authorization to operate from another world. That world is Heaven where our Lord and Savior Jesus Christ has reserved an eternal seat and position for us.

You know, sometimes we forget we are Heaven's citizens. This causes us to relate to this world as if it is our eternal place of position. But nothing could be further from the truth. We have to continue to remind ourselves that we have a command center that supersedes this natural world. A supernatural posture that we must hold to, no matter what.

I remember one day having to take my wife to the hospital and when it was time to speak to the specialist, the nursing staff rolled a cart into the room that had a television screen attached to it and the specialist spoke with my wife through the television screen. The specialist was operating from another place and space. Now, here is the interesting thing. They were assessing and giving orders from what seemed to me like another world. The doctor, my wife and the nursing staff who were caring for her all had remote access.

Well, for you and me, this is how we function. We operate from a totally different world and space than this earth realm. God reveals this to us in scripture. *"But God, who is rich in mercy, because of His great love with which He loved us, even when we were dead in trespasses, made us alive together with Christ (by grace you have been saved), and raised us up together, and made us sit together in the heavenly places in Christ Jesus."* Ephesians 2:4-6 NKJV

Understanding our position in Christ will help us continue to be the most influential people on planet Earth. The key word is understanding! We have to know in our core that this is not our home base. I have heard people say you cannot be so heavenly minded until you are no earthly good. However, I would like to say it like this. You cannot be so earthly minded until you are no heavenly good. We should always think like Heaven; especially if we say we are Kingdom citizens.

Proverbs 4:7 is another scripture we can stand on: *"Wisdom is the principal thing; Therefore, get wisdom. And in all your getting, get understanding."*

Now, this understanding we see here is not a worldly understanding. This is basically a mindset that says I am in total agreement with Heaven. If we are not careful, we can slip into a worldly understanding that will take our focus off of our true home base, which is Heaven. Therefore, we must hold fast to a mindset of being in total agreement with Heaven.

Proverbs 3:5-6 NKJV reminds us to… *"Trust in the LORD with all your heart, and lean not on your own understanding; In all your ways acknowledge Him, And He shall direct your paths."* Hallelujah! We are trusting in our God, who gives us the ability to operate from another world with the power He has given us before the foundation of the world.

If you and I could just wrap our minds around the fact that we are connected to a world that far outweighs this earth realm, we would dominate everything in this world. The sad thing is, many of us do not know or even believe we have the right to do such a thing.

The Real You

Listen, we do not have to wait until we die before we experience days of Heaven upon this Earth. We can take full advantage of this privilege right now. Yes, right now! We are called to rule and reign over everything on planet Earth. God, our Father, designed it that way. That is His plan and heart's desire for us, His sons and daughters. When we own up to who we really are and where we come from, things will become sweatless for us.

Most of us become extremely exhausted because we devalue the access that was granted to us by our Lord and Savior Jesus Christ to function and operate from another world, Heaven. It is our responsibility to remind ourselves of the citizenship we have in the heavenly realm. Also, we must keep in mind that the place we draw strength and confidence from is actually the place where we were birthed to take on this Kingdom mandate. This kingdom mandate is beckoning us to operate from another world.

Chapter 11
DIVINITY -VS- HUMANITY

"Walk in the spirit and you will not fulfill the lust of the flesh. The flesh and spirit are competing for your soul."

In my younger years of life, I did not know how important choosing the right path to take was for me where my soul was concerned. One thing I can vividly remember is I always felt there was some kind of tug of war going on inside of me, but I could never put my finger on it until later in life. It was the God in me verses the flesh suit that the God in me lives in (I hope I did not confuse you there) LOL!

This is comical to me now, but I did not understand it at the time. When my homies (friends) and I would partake in libations (alcoholic beverages) and certain medicinal drugs. I would talk about how wonderful and awesome God is and let them all know that Jesus loves them. This time of ministry may seem very odd to some people and I am quite sure it did to those whose high was just blown because they were reminded of the words spoken to them by a spirit filled parent or grandparent.

Out of all of these years, I have come to realize it was the divinity in me competing with the humanity side of me. I am so thankful I can say today my divinity wins out over my humanity most of the time. I'M JUST SAYING! (LOL)!

One thing we should all remember is our spirit and our flesh are always competing for our soul. This is a perpetual battle that goes on inside of all of us as long as we exist in this earth realm. One thing is for sure, we should always root for the spirit man who is *The Real You* to win over the flesh because our spirit never dies but it has a final destination, likewise so does the flesh.

We have two natures. Number one, we have a divine nature, our spirit. Number two, we have a human nature, our flesh. We all came out of God, who is spirit only. Therefore, we are spirit first, and it this is the case, and it is, that is the part of us we should allow to lead us. Our spirit is the God-part of who we are; it is God, our Heavenly Father's D.N.A. and should always override our earthly father's D.N.A.

Our divinity identifies you and me as Heavenly citizens who are on an assignment in the earth. So always remember you did not originate here, but you were transported here. As a matter of fact, we all are on a temporary visitation that has an unknown expiration date.

Let's not get it twisted! We need our humanity in order to function in this earth realm. However, we should view our human bodies as houses we need to live here. Let's revisit the astronaut in space analogy. Remember, if an astronaut wants to go into space, he will first need a space suit and second, he will need a spaceship. The astronaut is not the space suit or the spaceship he needs to get to his destination, but they both are essential for him to survive in space. Likewise, you are not your humanity, but it is essential for you to survive in the earth realm.

I think Galatians 5:16-26 NKJV says it best: *"I say then: Walk in the Spirit, and you shall not fulfill the lust of the flesh. For the flesh lusts against the Spirit, and the Spirit against the flesh; and these are contrary to one another, so that you do not do the things that you wish. But if you are led by the Spirit, you are not under the law. Now the works of the flesh are evident, which are: adultery, fornication, uncleanness, lewdness, idolatry, sorcery, hatred, contentions, jealousies, outbursts of wrath, selfish ambitions, dissensions, heresies, envy, murders, drunkenness, revelries, and the like; of which I tell you beforehand, just as I also told you in time past, that those who practice such things will not inherit the kingdom of God. But the fruit of the Spirit is love, joy, peace, longsuffering, kindness, goodness, faithfulness, gentleness, self-control. Against such there is no law. And those who are Christ's have crucified the flesh with its passions and desires. If we live in the Spirit, let us also walk in the Spirit. Let us not become conceited, provoking one another, envying one another."*

The Apostle Paul had a monumental struggle with his flesh trying to override his spirit man. The assignment of his life took him into many countries and situations. Paul was always faced with some type of challenge that would try to pull him out of his divinity and into his humanity. I noticed Paul would do something most people may not do, and that is; he talked to himself. If most of us would take time out and have honest conversations with ourselves, we could save ourselves a lot of trouble in the long run. Let's review what Paul had to say about the struggle he was having between his spirit man and his flesh, blood, and bone body in Romans 7:14-20 NKJV: *"For we know that the law is spiritual, but I am carnal, sold under sin. For what I am doing, I do not understand. For what I will to do, that I do not practice; but what I hate, that I do. If, then, I do what I will not to do, I agree with the law that it is good. But now, it is no longer I who do it, but sin that dwells in me. For I know that in me (that is, in my flesh) nothing good dwells; for to will is present with me, but how to perform what is good I do not find. For the good that I will to do, I do not do; but the evil I will not to do, that I practice. Now if I do what I will not to do, it is no longer I who do it, but sin that dwells in me."*

What the Apostle Paul was saying was, *"I'm having a serious struggle right now and I cannot seem to shake it!"* You may feel the same way, but beloved of God, we are already set up to win!

After we accept Jesus as our Lord and personal Savior, we receive what is called a recreated spirit or born-again spirit. Before Jesus died on the cross, He said three very important words: IT IS FINISHED! You may be asking yourself what was finished? Our victory over the temptations of the flesh was finished! I know you may say, but I have been giving in to the desires of my flesh most of my life. My friend, that is only by choice. *The Real You* (your spirit man) is ready, willing, and able to override the cravings of your flesh.

What happens to most of us is we allow our soul to go with our flesh because our flesh can mostly relate to what this physical world is presenting to us on a daily basis. This is why it is so important that we feed our spirit (divinity) daily. We cannot feed our flesh (humanity) daily and forget about our spirit. We will find ourselves living an unbalanced life. Your spirit allows you to be a god in the earth. Do not take my word for it. Read it for yourself in Psalms 82:6 NKJV: *"I said, You are gods, And all of you are children of the Most High."*

God said that about us because that is who we really are, but most people do not believe it. So they do not function in it! We must allow this truth to become the center of who we are and the core of what we believe. My friend, I want to encourage you to assume and hold your position in what and who God called and created you to be. Never be afraid or ashamed to embrace your true God-given identity.

I would like to take a moment to challenge you to make this confession: "I am just like God! My Heavenly Father created me as His perfect offspring! I am created to rule, reign and have dominion here in the earth. Therefore, I will not move out of my god-ship position! I embrace my Divinity so I can function just like Jesus here in the earth! I am a god!"

If that last statement "I am a god" made you feel some kind of way, that is because your humanity is fighting to distract you from embracing your divinity. So, maybe if we can hear and see it from the mouth of Jesus, in John 10:34 NKJV, it will sink in: *"Jesus answered them, Is it not written in your law, I said, You are gods?"*

You see, Jesus himself confirmed our true nature and identity. By our Lord and Savior's own admission, our identity has been confirmed. He was revealing to the people during that time their true identity and the same is true for you and me.

So, no matter what the Devil or anyone says, never allow them to convince you to doubt or question the real you! The YOU God says you are!

CONFESSIONS:

Use the space below to write your own confessions about *The Real You*.

Eddie J. Scarbrough

The Real You

www.ingramcontent.com/pod-product-compliance
Lightning Source LLC
Chambersburg PA
CBHW051552010526
44118CB00022B/2672